Who Was
Thomas Alva Edison?

THOMAS ALVA EDISON

Who Was
Thomas Alva Edison?

By Margaret Frith

Illustrated by John O'Brien

Grosset & Dunlap

For David, ever curious—M.F.
For Linda—J.O.

GROSSET & DUNLAP
Published by the Penguin Group
Penguin Group (USA) Inc., 375 Hudson Street, New York, New York 10014, U.S.A.
Penguin Group (Canada), 10 Alcorn Avenue, Toronto, Ontario, Canada M4V 3B2
(a division of Pearson Penguin Canada Inc.)
Penguin Books Ltd, 80 Strand, London WC2R 0RL, England
Penguin Ireland, 25 St Stephen's Green, Dublin 2, Ireland (a division of Penguin Books Ltd)
Penguin Group (Australia), 250 Camberwell Road, Camberwell, Victoria 3124, Australia
(a division of Pearson Australia Group Pty Ltd)
Penguin Books India Pvt Ltd, 11 Community Centre, Panchsheel Park,
New Delhi-110 017, India
Penguin Group (NZ), Cnr Airborne and Rosedale Roads, Albany, Auckland 1310,
New Zealand (a division of Pearson New Zealand Ltd)
Penguin Books (South Africa) (Pty) Ltd, 24 Sturdee Avenue, Rosebank,
Johannesburg 2196, South Africa

Penguin Books Ltd, Registered Offices: 80 Strand, London WC2R 0RL, England

Text copyright © 2005 by Margaret Frith. Illustrations copyright © 2005 by John O'Brien.
Cover illustration copyright © 2005 by Nancy Harrison. All rights reserved. Published by
Grosset & Dunlap, a division of Penguin Young Readers Group, 345 Hudson Street,
New York, New York 10014. GROSSET & DUNLAP is a trademark of
Penguin Group (USA) Inc. Printed in the U.S.A.

Library of Congress Cataloging-in-Publication Data

Frith, Margaret.
Who was Thomas Alva Edison? / by Margaret Frith ; illustrated by John O'Brien.
p. cm.
Includes bibliographical references.
ISBN 978-0-448-43765-1 (pbk.)
1. Edison, Thomas A. (Thomas Alva), 1847-1931—Juvenile literature. 2. Inventors—United
States—Biography—Juvenile literature. 3. Electric engineers—United States—Biography—
Juvenile literature. I. O'Brien, John, 1953- II. Title.
TK140.E3F736 2005
621.3'092—dc22

2005003386

20 19 18 17

Contents

Who Was
Thomas Alva Edison?

One day the Edisons couldn't find six-year-old Al, as his family called him. They were visiting Al's older sister and her husband on their farm. It was just outside of Milan, Ohio. The year was 1853.

Suddenly Al's uncle had an idea. He ran out to the barn and there he found Al sitting on a pile of straw. He was trying to hatch a goose egg. He had seen a hen sitting on her eggs when some baby chicks came out. Al wanted to make a baby goose come out of the egg.

The Edisons weren't surprised. They had three other children, but their youngest, Al, was the most curious. He would be that way all of his long life.

The world was very different when Thomas Alva Edison was a child—no electric light to see by, no recorded music to listen to, no movies to watch. It was Edison who made all of these possible and much more, changing our lives forever. Edison firmly believed in inventions, ones that could make everyday life easier and more comfortable. That is exactly what he accomplished.

Thomas Alva Edison was, perhaps, the greatest inventor of his time.

Chapter 1
Always Curious

Thomas Alva Edison was born on February 11, 1847, on a cold snowy night in Milan, Ohio.

His parents, Nancy and Samuel, named him Thomas after his great-uncle and Alva after Captain Alva Bradley, a good friend of his father. The family didn't call him Tom or Tommy. They called him Al.

Little Al wanted to find out everything about the world around him. He went about it like a scientist doing an experiment. He didn't just ask questions; he liked to find out the answers himself.

Once Al broke open a bumblebee's nest to see what was inside.

Another time he watched birds eat worms and fly off. So Al made a mixture out of water and mashed worms. Then he gave it

to a neighbor girl to drink. He wanted to see if eating worms would make her fly. But it just made her sick, and Al got a licking with a birch branch.

Nothing stopped Al—not bees, not a licking, not even falling into a grain-storage bin. He was walking around the rim of the bin when he fell in. Luckily someone pulled him out by the legs just before he was buried under the wheat.

Al's father owned a small grain and timber mill in Milan. Boats like Captain Alva Bradley's carried

timber down from Canada across Lake Erie, down the Huron River and through the Milan Canal. There it was cut into logs and planks at mills like Mr. Edison's.

Trucks and cars had not yet been invented, and trains didn't come to Milan. But one day a railroad line was built. Trains started chugging into town, and the canal wasn't so important anymore. The railroads were faster and easier to use for carrying things around the country. So when Al was seven, the

family moved to a new home in Port Huron, Michigan, more than a hundred miles north of Milan.

They lived in a big house on the St. Clair River. Al's father did lots of things to earn a living. He worked as a carpenter. He ran a grocery store. He had a vegetable garden. He tried farming. He even built a 100-foot tower overlooking the river. For twenty-five cents, anyone could climb up and watch the boats go by.

The Edisons had only been there a short time when Al caught scarlet fever. It was a serious illness back then without the medicines used today. He ran a high fever. A red rash broke out on his skin. Al got better, but he realized that he couldn't hear as well as he used to, probably because of the scarlet fever.

In school, the teacher complained that Al didn't pay attention. He would drift off. Maybe he was bored, or maybe he just couldn't hear everything.

One day eight-year-old Al heard his teacher telling someone that he was "addled." He meant Al's brain was scrambled. When Al told his mother, she was furious. She took him out of school and began teaching him at home.

Al loved to read. How surprised his teacher would have been to see the difficult books his

VOLTA'S BATTERY

FIRST ELECTRIC BATTERY STACK OF
COPPER AND ZINC DISCS SEPARATED
BY SALTWATER-SOAKED CLOTH

mother gave to him. Books about history, nature, and science. He read them just as fast as he could. One book was a favorite. It was called *A School Compendium of Natural and Experimental Philosophy*. It was a science book. It talked about electricity, batteries, electrical toys, and a lot more. It had simple experiments.

Al got so excited, he started doing experiments all over the house. He used stuff like feathers, beeswax, and chemicals from the drugstore. His bedroom was full of jars and bottles. Finally his mother sent him to the basement to set up his own lab.

MORSE CODE

(1791–1872)

SAMUEL MORSE WAS BORN IN CHARLESTOWN, MASSACHUSETTS. HE WAS A PORTRAIT PAINTER FOR THE FIRST HALF OF HIS LIFE.

MORSE WAS ALWAYS INTERESTED IN SCIENCE, ESPECIALLY ELECTRICITY. HE WAS FORTY-ONE YEARS OLD WHEN HE HAD AN IDEA. WHAT ABOUT SENDING MESSAGES IN CODE THROUGH A WIRE? THE IDEA CAME TO HIM WHILE HE WAS ON A SHIP, TRAVELING HOME FROM FRANCE, WHERE IT HAD TAKEN A WHOLE MONTH FOR A LETTER TO REACH HIM FROM AMERICA.

THE SIMPLE INSTRUMENT HE BUILT IN 1837 WORKED THE VERY FIRST TIME. BUT IT WASN'T UNTIL 1844 THAT HE COULD SEND THE FIRST "OFFICIAL" TELEGRAM. MORSE TAPPED OUT WORDS FROM THE BIBLE: "WHAT HATH GOD WROUGHT?" IT WENT FROM WASHINGTON, D.C., TO BALTIMORE, MARYLAND, THIRTY-FOUR MILES AWAY. IT TOOK LESS THAN A SECOND TO TRAVEL THROUGH THE WIRE.

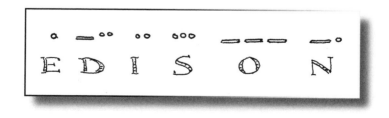

One part in the book interested Al most of all. It was about Morse's telegraphic alphabet. Morse was the name of a code. It was used to send messages over telegraph wires. There were no telephones yet. You couldn't talk to someone far away. But you could send messages that reached them quickly.

Samuel Morse made up the code. Instead of using letters and numbers, he used dots and dashes to send messages that became known as telegrams.

The railroad played a big part because the telegraph wires that carried telegrams were strung on poles along the railroad tracks. An operator in a railroad station could wire ahead if schedules changed, or if there was an accident or a delay of some kind. Telegraphy made the trains safer.

An operator tapped out a message of dots and dashes with a metal key on a board. The message raced along a wire as electrical pulses to the next station. The dots and dashes were notched, or cut, into a roll of paper. An operator decoded the message using Morse code, and wrote down the message in words.

Telegrams were expensive, so mostly businesses sent them. But people sent them too for news they wanted to get to their families and friends fast, like the birth of a new baby.

Al couldn't wait to try it. He made a simple telegraph key, and he began learning Morse code. He even set up a wire between his house and a friend's house nearby. As they learned the code they began sending messages back and forth.

Soon Al would go to work on the railroad. It was there that his interest in telegraphy grew much more serious.

Chapter 2
Young Inventor

Al was twelve when his father helped him get a job on the Grand Trunk Railroad. The train traveled back and forth between Port Huron and Detroit, Michigan, every day.

Al was a newsboy. Along with other boys, he sold newspapers, magazines, and snacks like candy and peanuts or sandwiches. The train didn't have a

dining car. The passengers had to bring their own food or buy it from the boys.

The train left Port Huron at seven in the morning and returned at nine in the evening. It was a three-hour journey each way. Al had lots of time in Detroit before the trip back home.

Al was not a boy to sit around and do nothing. He spent time at the library reading, mostly science books. He also began to dream up other ways to make money on the train. He bought things from the Detroit market and sold them to train riders on the way home to Port Huron. In Port Huron he took vegetables from his family's farm and sold them at the station.

Then in Detroit he noticed that a newspaper was throwing out ink, paper, and old pieces of type. Al bought a small printing press and started a weekly newspaper. He called it the *Grand Trunk Herald*. A subscription cost eight cents a month. He sold about two hundred copies a week. People liked it because it carried local news, train schedules, ads— and gossip.

Al set up his printing press right there in the baggage car on the train. He also set up a simple lab. He wrote. He printed. He did experiments. The conductor didn't mind.

Then one day, one of his chemical mixtures caught fire. The conductor did mind now! He was really angry with Al. He picked him up and threw him off the train along with all his stuff. But

ABRAHAM LINCOLN

Al didn't lose his job as a newsboy. He just couldn't have a lab on the train anymore.

In 1861, the Civil War broke out between the North and the South. Michigan was on the side of the North, the side of the president, Abraham Lincoln. People were particularly anxious for news. It was not long before Al saw a way to sell even more newspapers. He got a telegraph operator in Detroit to wire the war news of that day ahead to the stations on the way to Port Huron. Operators wrote the news on a chalkboard at the station. By the time the train arrived, people had heard what was happening, and they wanted to read more about the events of the day in the newspaper. Al usually sold about a hundred papers. On the day when the sad news came of the terrible battle at Shiloh, Tennessee, where more than 23,000 men were killed or wounded, he sold one thousand newspapers.

Al was a teenager now, and he decided he wanted to be called Tom. From then on he was known as Tom or Thomas.

One day Tom saw a train about to hit the stationmaster's three-year-old son, Jimmy. He dashed onto the tracks and pulled him to safety.

As thanks, the stationmaster offered to teach Tom about telegraphy. Tom was thrilled. He already knew Morse code. Here was a chance to learn how to become a real telegraph operator.

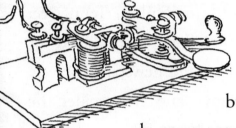

By now telegrams were not only sent from railroad stations, but from offices owned by a company called Western Union. Tom worked hard and soon he had a new job. He was just sixteen when he went to work for Western Union in Port Huron.

Later, Tom took jobs with Western Union in other cities. He went from one place to the next. He was getting faster and faster at sending and receiving messages. A good telegrapher could send or receive about forty-five words a minute.

Tom wanted to be the best. He practiced at night in his room. He liked to tap out plays, like *Hamlet*, by William Shakespeare.

One day a friend told Tom about a job at Western Union in Boston, Massachusetts. It was 1868. The Civil War had ended three years before. Now Tom was twenty-one years old. Off he went.

Tom worked at night. During the day he worked on his inventions. He spent time at a machine shop where they could make the parts he needed

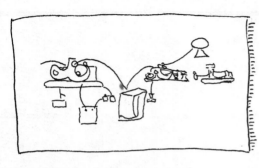

to build whatever he was working on. This meant that Tom didn't get much sleep. This habit stayed with him all his life.

Tom always carried a small notebook in his pocket so he could jot down ideas. The first invention he made that he thought he could sell was an electric voting machine. He had noticed how long it took lawmakers in the Massachusetts legislature to vote. Each vote was written by hand. An electric machine would make voting much faster.

Tom applied for a patent from the U.S. government in Washington, D.C. A patent protects the owner of an idea for an invention. It stops someone else from copying it and selling it. The owner gives the date, time, and place where the idea began. The patent also includes a description and sketches of the idea. It stays on file whether the owner makes the invention or not. Over sixty years' time Tom was granted 1,093 patents—more than anybody else, even to this day.

ELECTRONIC VOTE COUNTER

Tom tried to sell his voting machine to the state. But the lawmakers didn't want it. They were glad that voting took a long time. This way, they could try and persuade others to change their vote before the voting was over.

Tom even went to Washington, D.C., to see if the U.S. Congress wanted it. For the same reason, they didn't.

Tom couldn't believe it. He decided right then that he would never make any invention unless he was sure people wanted it. It was the only way to make money. Tom didn't want to be an inventor to become rich. But he understood that it took money to make his ideas happen.

Tom wrote articles about telegraphy. People read them and admired the young inventor. Many called him a genius. Some even wanted to give him money to help him invent things. They were called investors.

So Tom quit his job at Western Union. Now he would spend all of his time inventing. He wanted to figure out how to send more than one message over a wire at a time so that more telegrams could be sent. But after only a year, Tom had run out of money. He decided it was time to leave Boston and move to New York City.

Chapter 3
Tom and His "Boys"

In 1869 Tom arrived in New York without a job. But Tom had no trouble finding one. He was already known and respected as a smart young man with exciting, original ideas. He was someone who could make things.

NEW YORK CITY — 1870S

Tom had no problem finding work. After a while, he and a fellow worker started their own business. Making and developing new machines—that's what they would do. The company's most successful machine was called the universal stock printer. All day long it sent the changing price of gold to businesses on Wall Street. Tom had developed the printer, and he sold the patent for it to Western Union for thirty thousand dollars. With this money and

UNIVERSAL STOCK PRINTER

two investors, Tom started his own company in 1870. He found a large building in Newark, New Jersey, for his Newark Telegraph Works. He continued working on his inventions. But the company also manufactured, or made, machines to sell. Tom was always working to improve any kind of machine. And companies like Western Union came to him to make a machine they needed, or to fix problems with machines they already used.

Working for Tom meant working long hours. He was at the office in Newark all the time. He knew everything that was happening. He kept detailed notes. He made sketches of his new ideas. He worked harder than anyone. Tom believed from his own experience that doing something yourself, like making a machine, was the best way to learn.

One day a young woman named Mary Stilwell came to work at the company. She and Tom fell in love. She was sixteen. He was twenty-four. Three months later, they married on Christmas Day. But even on that day, Tom went to

MARY STILWELL

work for a few hours, and Mary quickly found out that Tom would spend much more time at work than at home.

Over the years the Edisons had three children. First came Marion and Thomas Jr. Their father fondly called them Dot and Dash, after Morse code. Then came another son, William. Tom loved his family, but still he spent more time at work than at home. This was not so easy for Mary and the children. Often his wife was lonely and frustrated.

Most inventors worked alone. Tom was different. He liked working with a team as long as he was the boss. He hired the best men he could find. He needed draftsmen who could draw his ideas on paper, machinists who could make things from his sketches, and men who understood what he was trying to do and come up with improvements of their own.

Tom called them "The Boys." They called him "The Old Man," even though he was only twenty-four years old and younger than many of them. A few of his "Boys" worked with Tom for twenty or thirty years.

In these early years, Tom figured out a way to send four telegraph messages at once—two in one direction and two in the other. Someone else had

already figured out how to send and receive two messages, but four meant twice the messages in less time. He called it the quadruplex.

ELECTRIC PEN

He also perfected an electric pen. The writer
"wrote" a message with the pen. A small motor
powered by a battery moved the point of the pen
up and down, punching small holes into paper to
make a kind of stencil. Then the paper with the
message on it could be inked onto other pieces of
paper with a roller. The message could be printed
over and over again.

After six years in Newark, Tom felt that it was time for a change again. He wanted to spend more time inventing instead of manufacturing. He found a small farming community in New Jersey called Menlo Park. It was about twenty-five miles from New York City. It was just the right place for his family and his "Boys"—about a dozen of them.

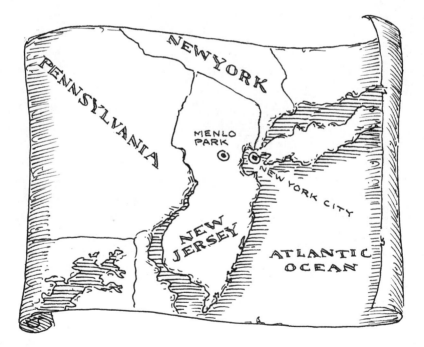

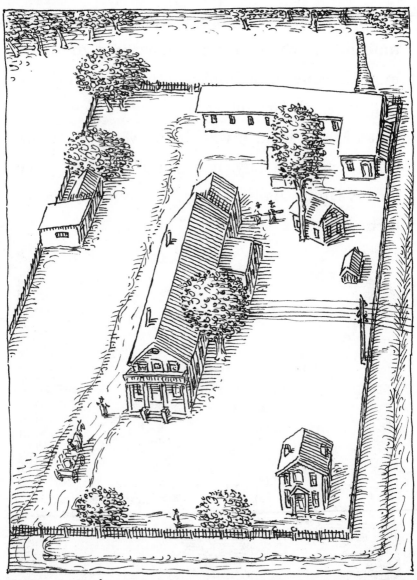

EDISON'S MENLO PARK COMPOUND

In 1876 Tom bought two large plots of land and began planning and building. He had a two-story building for his laboratory. The office and a library were in another building. There was a carpentry shop, a machine shop, a glassblowing shed, and an engine house. He even built a boardinghouse where his "Boys" could live.

Tom had a lovely large house built for the family. But having them nearby didn't mean that Tom was home more. He was rarely home for dinner, even when he promised Mary he'd be there, and never home for lunch.

Young Marion sometimes got to take her father's lunch to him in his lab. She was the lively,

curious one. Unfortunately her brother, Thomas Jr., was often sick.

Sometimes Marion found her father going over work with his "Boys." Sometimes she'd find him sitting at his simple table facing away from the bustle going on around him. If she was lucky, Tom might give his "Dot" a dime to buy candy.

Marion loved to visit. Everywhere she looked were strange half-built contraptions on the worktables, shelves packed with jars and bottles, and cubbyholes full of feathers, stones, and other interesting materials.

Tom and his "Boys" loved Menlo Park. They were glad to be away from the bustle of Newark. They didn't even mind when Tom removed all the springs from the clocks so that no one would pay any attention to what time it was.

They still worked long hours, but it was on "Tom's time." Sometimes Tom never got home at all. He'd sleep in his clothes on a

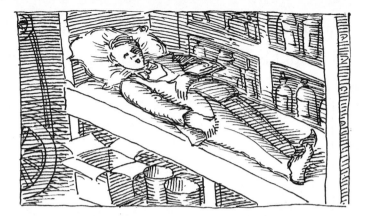

bench in the lab for a few hours and then go back to work.

Menlo Park was the perfect place to think. Tom once said, "The man who doesn't make up his mind to cultivate the habit of thinking cannot make the most of himself. All progress, all success, springs from thinking." He called Menlo Park his "invention factory." His teams of "Boys" worked on as many as forty projects at a time.

The more successful Tom became, the more attention he got. Investors came to see him. Magazines and newspapers wrote articles about him and his inventions.

Tom liked the publicity. The more that people heard about his inventions, the more people would want them.

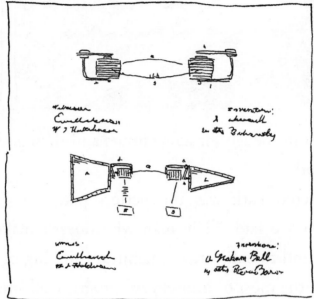

BELL'S TELEPHONE DIAGRAM

It was around this time that Alexander Graham Bell invented the telephone. Tom wished he had thought of it first. So did Western Union. They wanted their own telephone to compete with Mr. Bell's. They worried that the telephone might replace the telegraph.

THE TELEPHONE

THE FAMOUS INVENTOR OF THE TELEPHONE, ALEXANDER GRAHAM BELL, WAS BORN IN SCOTLAND LESS THAN A MONTH AFTER EDISON WAS BORN. HIS MOTHER, A TALENTED PIANIST AND PAINTER, WAS ALMOST TOTALLY DEAF. HIS GRANDFATHER, HIS FATHER, AND BELL HIMSELF TAUGHT DEAF PEOPLE. HIS FATHER INVENTED "VISIBLE

(1847–1922)

SPEECH," AN ALPHABET OF SYMBOLS, WHICH HELPED THE DEAF LEARN TO TALK.

BELL MOVED TO BOSTON IN 1871. HE WAS INTERESTED IN ELECTRICITY AND, LIKE EDISON, WORKED SUCCESSFULLY ON IMPROVING THE TELEGRAPH. THIS LED HIM TO THE INVENTION OF THE TELEPHONE IN 1876. HE SPOKE THE FIRST WORDS TO HIS ASSISTANT, WHO WAS IN ANOTHER ROOM. "WATSON, COME HERE. I WANT YOU."

But Bell's telephone had problems. It only worked over short distances, and you had to shout really loud to be heard. Western Union asked Tom to come up with a better telephone.

What the telephone needed was a different transmitter. That's the part that transmits, or sends, the voice from one phone to another. It is located in the part of the phone that a person talks into. When the sound of the voice reaches the transmitter, it vibrates, or moves back and forth. Sound is changed into electricity, which can travel long distances over a wire.

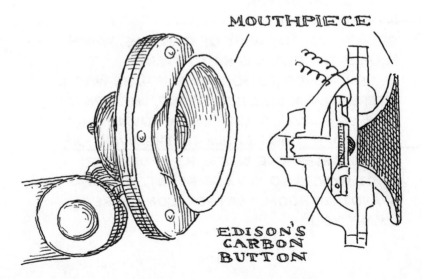

MOUTHPIECE

EDISON'S
CARBON
BUTTON

Bell's transmitter was made of metal, and that was the problem. It didn't make strong enough vibrations. Tom had to find out what material would work better than metal.

This took time. Tom and his team worked day and night. It was Tom who came up with the answer.

One day Tom scraped some carbon off a broken piece of glass from an oil lamp. Carbon, or lampblack, is the black soot a candle or an oil lamp gives off.

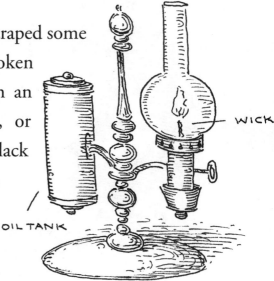

WICK

OIL TANK

OIL LAMP

Tom rolled the carbon between his fingers as if it were soft clay. He made two button shapes. He put one on Bell's metal transmitter and one right next to it, almost touching it. When they vibrated, the electrical current carried a strong, clear signal over the phone wire. Problem solved!

Tom was disappointed that he didn't invent the telephone. But his carbon transmitter made telephones work better. And his transmitter led him to a wonderful invention of his own. No one had yet come up with a way of recording and playing back a person's voice. Tom was about to do it. His invention was called the phonograph.

Chapter 4
His Invention Factory

In the mid 1800s, a man in France and a man in Massachusetts both came up with ways to record sound—but as a pattern on paper much the way the dots and dashes of Morse code look on paper.

Nobody had figured out how to record sounds and play them back so they could be heard again. That's what Tom wanted to do. He had an idea. But he didn't know if it would work. He had drawn some rough sketches. But that was all.

For eight months Tom and his team kept working on his idea for a phonograph. They were working on other inventions too. They were not in a big hurry. But then an article appeared in an important magazine, *Scientific American*. It said that Thomas Edison had invented an amazing machine. It played the human voice. "A wonderful invention," they announced with great fanfare. Tom knew that everyone would be asking to hear his amazing phonograph.

Now Tom was in a big hurry.

Had someone at Menlo Park told a reporter about what Tom was working on? Maybe. Tom didn't mind. Maybe he even knew who had told the magazine about the phonograph. He liked publicity. But now he had to make his phonograph. And soon.

It was November 1877. Tom sat down and did another rough sketch. He gave it to his best machinist. Anyone else might look at his drawing and wonder how to follow it. But this machinist was used to Tom's sketches. A week later he came back with a model.

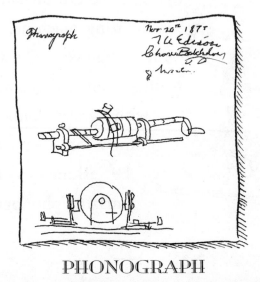

PHONOGRAPH

The model had a long screw with a handle at one end. The screw ran through the middle of a metal cylinder wrapped in tinfoil. On either side of the cylinder was a metal disk with a pin and a short hollow tube.

Tom leaned toward the machine, turned the handle, and spoke into one of the tubes as the cylinder moved along the screw. "Mary had a little lamb. Its fleece was white as snow. And everywhere that Mary went, the lamb was sure to go."

The sound of Tom's voice made the metal disk

with the pin vibrate and scratch a sound pattern on the tinfoil. When he stopped speaking, Tom pulled the pin away from the cylinder. He turned the handle in the opposite direction and moved the cylinder back to where it had been. He put the pin on the other side against the cylinder.

HOW THE PHONOGRAPH WORKS

TO RECORD: SOUND ENTERS HORN, VIBRATES A DIAPHRAGM WITH A NEEDLE THAT CAUSES INDENTATIONS ON A TURNING CYLINDER COVERED WITH TINFOIL.

TO PLAY BACK: THE INDENTATIONS ON THE CYLINDER VIBRATE A NEEDLE AND DIAPHRAGM ON THE OPPOSITE SIDE AND THE SOUND EXITS HORN.

Now was the big moment. Tom turned the handle again. The cylinder moved along the screw and out came his voice speaking the lines of the familiar nursery rhyme.

Tom was almost as surprised as everyone else. He could hardly believe that his phonograph worked the very first time.

Tom went to the offices of *Scientific American* to play his wonderful phonograph. The excited editors crowded around. Wow! They had never seen—or heard—anything like it.

In April 1878, Tom traveled to Washington, D.C. There he spoke to the National Academy of Sciences about his invention. He also had his photograph taken by Matthew Brady, the famous Civil War photographer.

MATTHEW BRADY

MATTHEW BRADY STUDIED PHOTOGRAPHY IN NEW YORK CITY UNDER SAMUEL MORSE, THE INVENTOR OF THE TELEGRAPH. HE PHOTOGRAPHED LOTS OF FAMOUS AMERICANS, INCLUDING ABRAHAM LINCOLN. HE TOOK ONE PICTURE RIGHT BEFORE LINCOLN BECAME PRESIDENT. IT TOOK BRADY ABOUT

(1823–1896)

FIFTEEN SECONDS TO TAKE THE PHOTOGRAPH. LINCOLN HAD TO WEAR A CLAMP TO HOLD HIS HEAD PERFECTLY STILL. OTHERWISE, THE PHOTO WOULD LOOK BLURRY.

DURING THE CIVIL WAR, BRADY WAS THE FIRST PHOTOGRAPHER TO TAKE PICTURES OF BATTLEFIELDS.

After a long day of meetings and receptions, President Rutherford B. Hayes asked Tom to come to the White House. It was eleven o'clock at night by the time he got there. The president was so impressed with Tom's

RUTHERFORD B. HAYES

phonograph that he made Mrs. Hayes get out of bed to hear it.

At first Tom thought companies would use his phonograph in business. He saw it as a kind of dictating machine for writing letters. Businesses did use it. It was called the Ediphone.

But during his lifetime Tom saw his phonograph's

popularity grow in ways he hadn't expected.

There was a big demand for music—in concert halls and in penny arcades. For five cents, several people could listen to a song at the same time. Soon people wanted their own phonographs at home.

LISTENING TUBES

Years later Tom wrote an article about all the ways the phonograph might be used one day. He saw far into the future. He even predicted audiotapes. He called them "talking books."

Tom was always working on more than one idea at a time. Perhaps he didn't pay as close attention to his phonograph as he should have. His company, the Edison Speaking Phonograph Company in New York City, made and sold phonographs using his

THE WIZARD
OF MENLO PARK

cylinders. But other companies went on to develop a more popular machine. It used flat disks called records.

Tom was only thirty years old when he invented his phonograph. At that young age, he became known as "The Wizard of Menlo Park."

The phonograph may have been Tom's "baby"— and his favorite. But it was the next invention that made him far more famous. Tom was about to work on something that would change the way people live forever.

Chapter 5
Turning on the Light

It was the summer of 1878. Tom had been working hard for a long time. He was thinking about taking a vacation. Then a friend invited him to join a group of scientists. They were traveling by train to Wyoming to see an eclipse of the sun.

Tom decided to go. He had been working on a machine he called a tasimeter for measuring temperature. He saw the trip as a chance to try it out.

Tom enjoyed talking to other scientists. After the eclipse, he and his friend traveled on together by train. It is said that Tom persuaded the train engineer to let him ride on the cowcatcher—the metal grate on the front of the train. This way Tom had the best view of the spectacular scenery

until the train came to a tunnel and he had to get back inside the car.

At this point in his life, Tom wasn't sure what he would work on next. On this trip out west, he stood and looked at the Platte River rushing by. He wondered out loud to his friend why the power of the river's flow couldn't be used to provide electricity to miners nearby. They were drilling for ore by hand, and it was obviously slow, hard work.

Tom's friend told him about a man he knew in Connecticut who had found an interesting way to use the power of electricity. He could send enough electricity to light up not just one arc light, but eight. An arc light makes light when an electric current jumps across the space between two carbon rods. The problem is that the light is harsh and bright. Arc lights also threw off sparks and could start a fire indoors. They were better suited for using outdoors.

Up to now, indoor lighting came from candles, oil lamps, or gas lamps. None of them gave off enough light to do much after dark. Gaslight had been around since the early 1800s. But it was expensive. Gas lamps made walls black and dirty. Sometimes its smell caused headaches. Gas could be dangerous, too, if it leaked or exploded. Fires might start. Still, gaslight was popular because it was the best light available.

GASLIGHT

IN 1816, COAL GAS LAMPS LIT UP A STREET
IN BALTIMORE, MARYLAND. IT WAS THE FIRST
AMERICAN STREET TO HAVE GASLIGHTS. LATER,
LAMPS WERE USED INDOORS.

NATURAL GAS COMES RIGHT OUT OF THE
GROUND. A WELL TWENTY-SEVEN FEET DEEP
WAS DRILLED IN FREDONIA, NEW YORK, IN 1820.
GENERAL LAFAYETTE, A HERO OF THE AMERICAN
REVOLUTION, VISITED AND WAS SERVED A DINNER
COOKED ON A GAS STOVE IN A ROOM LIT BY
GASLIGHT. IT WAS A MARVEL IN ITS DAY!

It could be found in homes, offices, factories, and outdoors in larger towns and cities around the country.

Tom was eager to see how the man in Connecticut was using electricity to light up his eight arc lights. He was surprised and interested to find out that the man was not using batteries, but a small generator made of a magnet and coils of wire.

Tom was very impressed with the eight arc lights. But he went home knowing that if he was to succeed with electric light he had to develop a simple lightbulb, which gives off a bright, soft glow from a heated filament, or material, inside the bulb. This was known as incandescent lighting.

Tom was all fired up to work on electric light. He knew that other people around the world were working on this too. He wanted to be the first to succeed. But he knew that inventing a working lightbulb wasn't enough. He had to invent one

ARC LIGHT

    LIGHT IS PRODUCED WHEN AN ARC
OF ELECTRICITY JUMPS BETWEEN TWO
CHARGED CONDUCTORS. IT WAS TOO
BRIGHT, SMELLY, AND EXPENSIVE FOR
USE IN HOMES AND OFFICES.

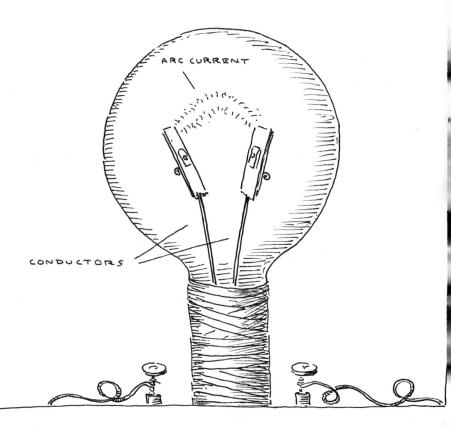

ARC CURRENT

CONDUCTORS

that could be sold at a price people could afford.

Tom also knew that he would have to figure out how to provide the electrical power to light up whole neighborhoods, whole cities—in fact, the whole country. That meant building power plants to provide the electricity.

Never shy about talking about his inventions, Tom wrote in his notebook: "The electric light is the light of the future, and it will be my light unless some other fellow gets up a better one."

It wasn't long before Tom was boasting to reporters that he would have his electric light ready in weeks. Not only that, he would build a power station on Pearl Street in Manhattan. It would bring electric light to a whole section of New York City! The area he chose was in the center of the city's financial district.

Why would Tom make such an announcement? He still had no idea how he would do this. Maybe he wanted to scare off other inventors. Maybe he did it to attract investors. Tom needed a lot of money to make this all happen.

Well, he got the money from rich men in New York City. Maybe this genius was about to put the gas companies out of business. The new electric lights might make lots of money. They didn't want to be left out. So before Tom even had anything to show, investors founded the Edison Electric Light Company.

Tom always loved having visitors at his lab in Menlo Park. He loved showing off his inventions, especially to reporters.

Now all that changed. He didn't want anyone coming over. He had bragged about electric light almost as if it existed already. And it didn't! He hadn't even applied for patents to protect his ideas.

Tom and his "Boys" settled in for some long, hard work.

First, and most importantly, they had to make a

bulb that was a vacuum. That meant no oxygen—a gas in the air we breathe—could be left inside the bulb. A filament will glow much longer if it heats up in a vacuum.

Tom hired a fantastic glassblower who could give him almost perfect, hollow bulbs. And, luckily, at about this time, a vacuum pump had been invented. It could suck almost all the air out of the bulbs.

The hardest task turned out to be finding the right filament, or material, that would carry the electric current and glow for a long time inside the bulb.

There were other problems too. The lights could not be wired in a series, or one to the other along the same wire. Why? If one went out, they all did.

Six weeks came and went. What about that neighborhood in New York, the one Tom said he was going to light up? Newspapers began writing stories accusing Tom of bragging.

Tom was still searching for the right filament. He tried so many materials—fish line, bamboo, spiderwebs, even the hair from one of his workers' head. For a while he thought that platinum was going to work. But even if it had, it would be too expensive to use.

Sometimes Tom would take time out to play a tune with two fingers on the organ he had put in the laboratory. Maybe it helped him think.

The "Boys" kept testing everything they could think of—over three thousand materials in all. Tom knew that finding out what did not work was as important as finding what did. A year and a half went by. Nothing.

But Tom did not give up, and one day he hit upon the answer. It was simple sewing thread covered in carbon and baked to just the right temperature.

On October 22, 1879, Tom's lightbulb glowed

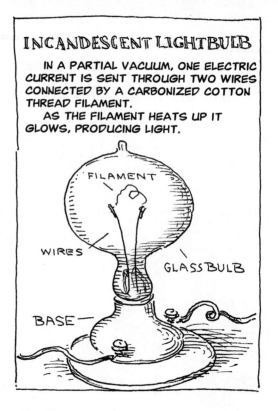

INCANDESCENT LIGHTBULB

IN A PARTIAL VACUUM, ONE ELECTRIC CURRENT IS SENT THROUGH TWO WIRES CONNECTED BY A CARBONIZED COTTON THREAD FILAMENT.

AS THE FILAMENT HEATS UP IT GLOWS, PRODUCING LIGHT.

FILAMENT

WIRES

GLASS BULB

BASE

for thirteen and a half hours. The next one glowed for over a hundred hours. Tom and his team were ecstatic. They had done it! Tom was only thirty-two years old.

Tom set up electric lights in Menlo Park for the December holiday season. They were powered by a new generator in the machine shop. It had two five-foot-high magnets and weighed over five hundred pounds.

Over three thousand people poured into Menlo Park to see what the "Wizard" had done now. They came by train and walked along the boardwalk to the laboratory. They looked up in amazement at the one hundred lamps glowing all along the way.

Once inside, they were stunned by the rooms lit with electric lights.

THE DYNAMO ROOM AT THE
PEARL STREET POWER STATION
NEW YORK CITY – SEPT 4, 1882

Now Tom turned to lighting up part of New York City. He needed a power plant, lines running underground, switches, meters, light fixtures, and many other things to keep his promise.

It would take another two and a half years, but on September 4, 1882, at three o'clock in the afternoon, a switch was thrown at the central station on Pearl Street. In the Wall Street offices of one of his important investors, Tom turned on all 106 new office lamps for the very first time. Tom knew that this was only a beginning. One day his electric light would be used all over the world.

Chapter 6
Making Moving Pictures

In 1884, at the height of his success, Tom suffered a terrible loss. His wife Mary died of an illness. She was only twenty-nine years old.

MINA MILLER

Tom had his children stay in New York City. His electricity business was there. He wanted to spend as much time as possible with Marion, now twelve; Thomas, now eight; and little William, who was only five.

Then, in 1885, Tom met a young woman named Mina Miller. Her family was from Ohio.

Mina's father was a millionaire businessman and inventor who had developed a very successful machine for harvesting grain. He himself received ninety-two patents in his lifetime.

Tom fell in love with Mina almost at once. She was interesting and educated. He even taught her Morse code so that they could "talk" to each other secretly, even among friends. It is said that Tom tapped out, "Will you marry me?" on the palm of her hand, and Mina tapped back, "Yes."

GLENMONT

Mina and Tom were married in 1886 and moved to a grand home, Glenmont, in West Orange, New Jersey. "It is a great deal too nice for me, but it isn't half nice enough for my little wife here," Tom said.

Tom and Mina were happy together. He was still at work as much as he had been when Mary was alive. But since Mina's father was also an inventor, perhaps she understood Tom's world better.

Still, it wasn't so easy for twenty-year-old Mina to become the young mother of three children. Nor was it easy for Marion, who was now fourteen and had become a companion to her father. Years later she said Mina "was too young to be a mother to me, but too old to be a chum."

Mina and Tom had three children, Madeleine, Charles, and Theodore. Holidays above all were

a time when Tom loved being at home with his large family. Mina planned lavish parties for Thanksgiving, Christmas, and Easter, but the Fourth of July was all Tom's. Everyone had to go outside very early—even before breakfast—for the fireworks that Tom had made himself. After breakfast and naps for the younger children, they rushed out for more activities, like picnics of watermelon and ice cream, and so it went on into the evening, ending with another enormous display of fireworks.

Unlike Mary, Mina loved having company. She gave large dinner parties, which Tom often tried to avoid by pretending to be sick. Their guest book was filled with the names of famous people—airplane pioneer Orville Wright, author and lecturer Helen Keller, who was blind and deaf from the age of two, and automobile maker Henry Ford. He wrote at the end of his stay, "Two of the best days I ever spent."

Moving to Glenmont made Tom decide to leave his Menlo Park laboratory. He built a new laboratory complex a mile from his home in West Orange. He wanted it to be the best in the world. "I will have the best-equipped and largest facility . . . for rapid and cheap development of an invention," Tom declared.

Tom had never forgotten his wish to give people what they wanted. Because of his great success with the electric light, he had the money, the power, and the influence to do it.

The West Orange complex opened in November 1887. It had a laboratory building three stories high. There was a physics lab, a chemistry lab, and a private lab just for Tom where he could focus and think without interruption.

But, for Tom, the center of West Orange was a large library with two galleries, a forty-foot ceiling, walls full of photographs and plaques, and shelves filled with ten thousand books and magazines from all around the world. Here Tom had his desk and a conference table. And it was here that Tom met the public—friends, investors, inventors, reporters, and editors.

West Orange was ten times larger than Menlo Park and at one time had as many as ten thousand workers. At any one time as many as thirty "companies" worked on projects, run by teams directed by Tom.

Along with new ideas, Tom never lost interest in improving his "baby," the phonograph. He might wander away from it and work on other inventions, but he always came back to it.

Not everything was a success. One of the things the "Boys" talked Tom into making was a talking doll for a Boston company. A small cylinder was put inside the two-foot-tall doll. A handle to turn the cylinder came out of her back. The talking doll worked fine in the factory, reciting poems and popular nursery rhymes. But when she reached the stores—nothing. All the thumping and bumping along the way had disturbed the mechanism. Most of the dolls never said a word.

In August 1889, Mina and Tom sailed to Paris for the Universal Exhibition. This was like a big fair for showing new products from many countries.

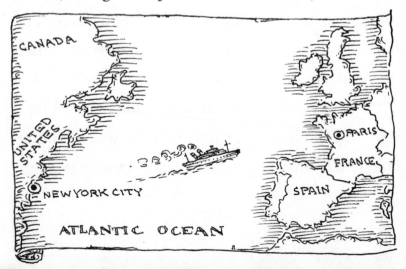

There was a huge Edison display. His phonograph was the most popular attraction. Only the new Eiffel Tower, the highest structure in the world at that time, had more visitors.

THE EIFFEL TOWER

"LA TOUR EIFFEL" STANDS 984 FEET HIGH OVER THE CITY OF PARIS. IT TOOK THREE HUNDRED MEN TWO YEARS TO BUILD IT. IT IS MADE OF FIFTEEN THOUSAND PIECES OF IRON HELD TOGETHER BY 2.5 MILLION RIVETS. IT CAN SWAY ALMOST FIVE INCHES IN STRONG WINDS. FORTY TONS OF PAINT ARE NEEDED TO COVER THE TOWER, WHICH REMAINED THE TALLEST STRUCTURE IN THE WORLD UNTIL 1930, WHEN THE CHRYSLER BUILDING, SOON FOLLOWED BY THE EMPIRE STATE BUILDING, WAS ERECTED IN NEW YORK CITY.

THE EIFFEL TOWER WAS COMPLETED IN 1889 FOR THE HUNDRED-YEAR ANNIVERSARY OF THE FRENCH REVOLUTION. GUSTAVE EIFFEL'S DESIGN WON THE COMPETITION FROM AMONG THE SEVEN HUNDRED ENTRIES SENT IN. SOME YEARS EARLIER, HE HAD DESIGNED THE IRON SKELETON FOR THE INSIDE OF THE STATUE OF LIBERTY, AND HE SUPERVISED THE RAISING OF THIS FAMOUS LADY IN NEW YORK HARBOR IN 1886.

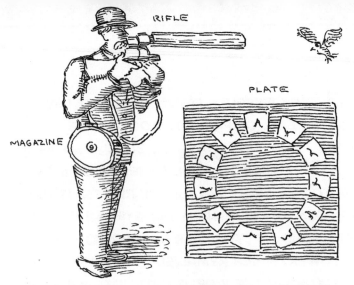

PHOTOGRAPHIC GUN

During this trip, Tom visited a Frenchman whose "photographic gun" had captured animals in motion, such as birds in flight.

Tom was interested in moving pictures. In October 1888 he had written, "I am experimenting upon

KINETOSCOPE

KINETOSCOPE PARLOR

an instrument which does for the Eye what the phonograph does for the Ear. . . . This apparatus I call a Kinetoscope—'Moving View.' "

Tom was a pioneer in developing a system for filming and showing moving pictures. His kinetograph was the camera, which took the pictures. His kinetoscope provided a way of looking at them.

In 1893 the first motion picture studio in America was built at West Orange. He named it the Black Maria.

PHOTOGRAPHY

LOUIS J M DAGUERRE

THE FIRST SUCCESSFUL PHOTOGRAPHIC PROCESS WAS THE DAGUERREOTYPE, NAMED AFTER FRENCHMAN LOUIS J. M. DAGUERRE, IN 1837. IT PRODUCED A DETAILED BLACK-AND-WHITE PICTURE AND WAS DESCRIBED AS A "MIRROR WITH A MEMORY."

THE NEXT IMPORTANT BREAKTHROUGH CAME IN 1851 WHEN A BRITISH PHOTOGRAPHER, FREDERICK SCOTT ARCHER, DISCOVERED A WAY TO MAKE AS MANY PRINTS AS HE WANTED TO OF AN IMAGE.

GEORGE EASTMAN

THEN, IN 1888, AMERICAN GEORGE EASTMAN INTRODUCED THE KODAK BOX CAMERA. IT WAS EASY TO CARRY AROUND, SO PHOTOGRAPHERS DIDN'T HAVE TO STAY IN AN INDOOR STUDIO WITH A DARKROOM NEARBY. IT WAS CHEAP AND EASY TO OPERATE, AND THE ROLL OF CELLULOID, OR PLASTIC, FILM COULD TAKE ONE HUNDRED BLACK-AND-WHITE PHOTOGRAPHS. THIS FILM MADE IT POSSIBLE FOR EDISON TO MAKE MOVING PICTURES.

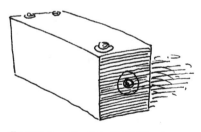

BOX CAMERA

About fifty feet long, the Black Maria was a weird-looking structure. It had a slanted roof that opened up with a pulley to let in the sun. It sat on

BLACK MARIA

a round platform with tracks like railroad tracks and moved around in a circle, following the path of the sun.

Filming in the Black Maria started in 1893. An early film showed a man sneezing, "performed" happily by a

"THE SNEEZE"

mechanic who worked at West Orange.

The first boxing match ever filmed starred heavyweight champion "Gentleman Jim" Corbett. Edison also filmed dance groups, acrobats, clowns, jugglers, and even the World's Strongest Man.

When Buffalo Bill's Wild West show came

BUFFALO BILL CODY

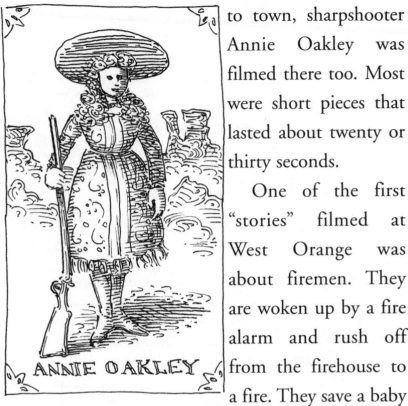

ANNIE OAKLEY

to town, sharpshooter Annie Oakley was filmed there too. Most were short pieces that lasted about twenty or thirty seconds.

One of the first "stories" filmed at West Orange was about firemen. They are woken up by a fire alarm and rush off from the firehouse to a fire. They save a baby and put out the fire. There wasn't any sound. Still, people were excited to look at it.

Tom's main interest in movies was in making better equipment, like his kinetoscope and his kinetograph. But as time went on, he drifted away to work on other ideas. He was not as closely involved as he had been with the phonograph and the lightbulb. He offered suggestions to his team, but he let them do a lot of the ideas and improvements without him. Eventually, he decided to get out of the movie business.

Chapter 7
Always Inventing

Tom was a man who never ran out of ideas. Although Tom was hard of hearing, he never lost his hearing completely. He didn't let it become a problem, even when his hearing got worse as he got older. In fact, he said it was a good thing because he could ignore noise swirling around him. He could concentrate on what was important to him. At one point Tom was told that an operation might cure his deafness. He didn't want it. And he was not interested in developing a hearing aid.

Tom found ways to work around his problem. He managed to "listen" to piano players trying out for his phonograph recordings by biting a metal plate attached to the piano. This allowed him to "hear" the music through the vibrations traveling through his jawbone. Was he "listening" through his teeth?

So much is known about Tom's work because of the records he kept. Over his seventy years of inventing, he filled four thousand notebooks and wrote and drew over three million notes, letters, and sketches.

Not all of Tom's ideas were successes. In 1891 he bought a mine in northwestern New Jersey. He wanted to find a way to produce low-grade iron ore by separating it from rock and sand. But after ten years he had to give up when rich deposits of high-grade iron ore were found in Minnesota. By this time Tom had lost millions of dollars.

Still, Tom's experience with mining led him to another business—cement. He came up with a way to pour a cement house in just six hours using molds and machinery that he developed in his mining business. His cement was used to build New York's Yankee Stadium and the Panama Canal.

Now it was the turn of the century. Automobiles were about to burst on the scene. Tom was convinced that an electric car would be the best car for the future. He set out to make a battery to run a car on electricity. He knew it would be cleaner than the gas that other inventors were trying. But he had to make a battery that would store enough electricity to run a car for a very long time. It also had to be cheap enough to make.

HENRY FORD

HENRY FORD

(1863–1947)

HENRY FORD WAS THE FIRST TO MAKE A CAR CHEAP ENOUGH FOR MOST AMERICANS TO BUY. IN 1908, HIS MOST POPULAR CAR, THE MODEL T, COST FIVE HUNDRED DOLLARS, AND HE HAD MORE ORDERS THAN HE COULD FILL. WITHIN TWO YEARS FORD CAME UP WITH HIS "ASSEMBLY LINE." WORKERS ASSEMBLED, OR PUT TOGETHER, EACH CAR. EACH MAN WORKED ON ONE PART ONLY. AS THE CAR TRAVELED ALONG A MOVING BELT, WORKERS ON EITHER SIDE ADDED THE NEXT PARTS NEEDED. AT THE END OF THE LINE A COMPLETE MODEL T WAS DRIVEN OFF, READY FOR A CUSTOMER. FORD MADE MODEL T'S FOR NINETEEN YEARS. HE SOLD OVER 15.5 MILLION OF THEM IN AMERICA.

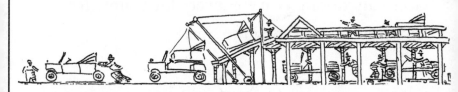

Tom finally came up with a good storage battery. But he was too late for cars. By 1903, Henry Ford was selling his gasoline-powered Model A to customers.

Tom's storage battery became very useful, even though it didn't power cars like Ford's. The navy used it to light ships and to power torpedoes. The railroad lit cars and signal lights with it. Some delivery trucks were powered by it. So were the lights on coal miners' helmets. Amazingly, the storage battery became his biggest moneymaker. Perhaps that surprised even Tom, who had once expected his phonograph "to grow up to be a big fellow and support me in my old age."

STORAGE
BATTERY

With all of Tom's successes, he was always ready to move on to the next idea. The same was true of his failures. He didn't look back and complain, and he never gave up until he had tried every possibility. Tom once said, "You come across anything you don't understand, you don't rest until you run it down. Most fellers try a few things and then quit. I never quit until I find what I'm after."

Tom worked in a time when many others were racing to think up and invent the next great idea. The world seemed alive with possibilities!

Tom understood work. He liked it. He once said, "Genius is one percent inspiration and ninety-nine percent perspiration." Of genius he said, "Sticking to it is the genius!" In 1914 a fire raged through some of his West Orange buildings. But even that did not discourage Tom. He started rebuilding immediately.

But even Tom could be narrow-minded. He

had nothing good to say about the radio. He was sure it wouldn't last.

As Tom got older, he didn't stop working. There are photographs of Tom in his seventies still going to West Orange. When he was sixty-five, he had a time clock installed. His workers punched in their cards to record the time they arrived and the time they left. So did Tom.

Over the years, Tom received many awards. In 1928 the U.S. Congress gave him a special medal for his lifetime of achievement. "I have accomplished all I promised," he said.

During the last fifteen years of Tom's life, he went on trips with old friends, among them Henry Ford, tire maker Harvey Firestone, and naturalist John Burroughs. They traveled to the

EDISON, FORD, BURROUGHS, FIRESTONE

Great Smoky Mountains, around New England, and to Michigan. They called their vacations together "camping trips." But they were well taken care of by the helpers who pitched their tents, took care of their clothes, and cooked their meals.

Tom and Mina spent time at the vacation home Tom had built soon after their marriage. It was in Ft. Myers, Florida. Of course, it had a laboratory.

During the last two years of his life, Tom suffered from a number of ailments, among them diabetes and a stomach ulcer, and his health declined. In

August 1931, he collapsed at Glenmont. He died on October 18 at the age of eighty-four. Mina lived another sixteen years.

Tom's funeral, on Wednesday, October 21, was private. But that evening, at the request of President Herbert Hoover, Americans turned off their lights at ten in the evening. For one minute, all over the United States, there was darkness in honor of Thomas Alva Edison, the man who lit up the world.

TIMELINE OF TOM'S LIFE

1847	Born in Milan, Ohio, on February 11
1854	The Edisons move to Port Huron, Michigan
1859	Works as a newsboy on the railroad
1863	Works as a telegraph operator in cities around the U.S.
1868	Moves to Boston, Massachusetts; invents an electric vote recorder and applies for his first patent
1869	Moves to New York City and develops a Universal Stock Printer
1870	Moves to Newark, New Jersey, to start a manufacturing and invention factory
1871	Marries Mary Stilwell on Christmas Day
1874	Develops quadruplex telegraph
1876	Moves to his new Menlo Park, New Jersey, laboratory to concentrate on inventing
1877	Develops carbon transmitter to improve the telephone; invents the phonograph
1879	Invents working electric lightbulb
1882	Brings electric light to a square mile of New York City from his Pearl Street power station
1884	Wife, Mary, dies
1886	Marries Mina Miller and buys Glenmont in West Orange, N.J.
1887	Builds his West Orange laboratory
1888	Develops the kinetograph and kinetoscope for motion pictures
1900	Begins working on storage battery for electric cars
1927	Works on a natural rubber project for car tires
1928	Receives a special medal from the U.S. Congress
1931	Dies on October 18

TIMELINE OF THE WORLD

First "official" telegram sent from Washington, D.C., to — **1844**
Baltimore, Maryland

Uncle Tom's Cabin by Harriet Beecher Stowe is published — **1851**

The Civil War — **1861-65**

President Abraham Lincoln is assassinated on April 14 — **1865**

A cable to send telegrams (and later telephone calls) is laid on — **1866**
the floor of the Atlantic Ocean between America and Europe

The transcontinental railroad joins East and West Coasts — **1869**

Alexander Graham Bell invents the first working telephone — **1876**

The Brooklyn Bridge linking Manhattan and Brooklyn — **1883**
is completed

The dedication of the Statue of Liberty in New York Harbor — **1886**

Eiffel Tower is completed in Paris, France — **1889**

The Wright Brothers make their first successful flight at — **1903**
Kitty Hawk, North Carolina

Admiral Peary is first to reach the North Pole on April 6 — **1909**

The *Titanic* sinks on its first voyage between Great Britain — **1912**
and America on April 14

World War I — **1914-18**

The Nineteenth Amendment gives women the right to vote — **1920**

Adolf Hitler becomes the Nazi Party leader in Germany — **1921**

The stock market crashes on Wall Street in New York City — **1929**
and brings on the Great Depression

BIBLIOGRAPHY

Buranelli, Vincent. **Thomas Alva Edison.** Silver Burdett Press, Englewood Cliffs, New Jersey, 1989.

Cousin, Margaret. **The Story of Thomas Alva Edison.** Random House, New York, 1965.

Delano, Marfé Ferguson. **Inventing the Future: A Photobiography of Thomas Alva Edison.** National Geographic, Washington, D.C., 2002.

Egan, Louise. **Thomas Edison: The Great American Inventor.** Barron's Educational Series, Inc., Hauppauge, New York, 1987.

Tagliaferro, Linda. **Thomas Edison: Inventor of the Age of Electricity.** Lerner Publications Company, Minneapolis, 2003.